DEPARTMENT OF THE NAVY
HEADQUARTERS UNITED STATES MARINE CORPS
3000 MARINE CORPS PENTAGON
WASHINGTON, DC 20350-3000

I0500601

MARINE CORPS SAFETY PROGRAM

MCO 5100.29B
SD
28 Jul 2011

MARINE CORPS ORDER 5100.29B

From: Commandant of the Marine Corps
To: Distribution List

Subj: MARINE CORPS SAFETY PROGRAM

Ref: (a) Public Law 91-596, "The Occupational Safety and Health (OSH)
           Act of 1970," December 29, 1970
       (b) 29 CFR 1960, Basic Program Elements for Federal Employee
           Occupational Safety & Health Programs and Related Matters
       (c) 29 CFR 1910, 1-398, Occupational Safety & Health Standards
       (d) DOD Instruction 6055.1, "DOD Safety and Occupational Health (SOH)
           Program," August 19, 1998
       (e) SECNAVINST 5100.10J
       (f) NAVMC DIR 5100.8
       (g) OPNAVINST 3750.6R

Encl: (1) Marine Corps Safety Program
       (2) List of Other Applicable Safety Program Policies and Resources

Reports Required: I.   Warrior Preservation Status Report (WPSR) (Report
                        Control Symbol MC-5100-05), para 4b(2)(f),
                        4b(14)(k) and encl (1), chap 4, para 3.
                   II. ANYMOUSE (Report Control Symbol MC 5100.06), encl (1),
                        chap 2, para 1m.
                   III. U.S. Marine Corps Ground Climate Assessment Survey
                        System (GCASS), i.e., Aviation Command Safety
                        Assessment (CSA), Aviation Maintenance Climate
                        Assessment Survey System (MCAS) or Ground Safety
                        Assessment Survey (Report Control Symbol MC-5100-07),
                        para 4b(2)(m), para 4b(14)(c), encl(1), chap 2, para
                        1n;chap 3, para 5b; and chap 3, para 5b(2).
                   IV. ORM Status Report (Report Control Symbol MC-5100-08),
                        encl (1), chap 3, para 5a(3).

1. Situation. Force preservation is a vital element of our combat
readiness; death, serious injury, and the loss of materiel assets due to
mishaps directly and negatively impacts the warfighting capability of the
entire Marine Corps. Engaged leadership at all levels is the key to ensuring
a command climate that demands the preservation of Marine Corps assets
through risk management. This Order and enclosure (1) establishes the
minimum requirements of the Marine Corps Safety Program based on the
references and policies required by resources listed in enclosure (2).

2. Cancellation. MCO 5100.29A.

3. Mission. Commands at all levels shall establish and maintain a vibrant
and viable safety program where maintaining combat readiness, eliminating

DISTRIBUTION STATEMENT A: Approved for public release; distribution is
unlimited.

preventable mishaps, and preserving our most precious assets — our Marines, Sailors, civilian personnel and equipment — is every Marine's goal and responsibility.

4. Execution

   a. Commander's Intent and Concept of Operations

      (1) Commander's Intent. To establish and maintain a safety culture throughout the Marine Corps that preserves all resources through risk management, reinforces on- and off-duty safe behavior, and results in an enhanced state of combat readiness.

      (2) Concept of Operations

         (a) Apply the safety standards promulgated by the references and this Order to all operations and workplaces.

         (b) The Marine Corps Safety Program shall apply to military-unique equipment, systems, operations, or workplaces, in whole or in part, as they apply to warrior preservation and mission accomplishment. When application of federal safety standards is not possible or when no regulatory standard exists for such military application, the Marine Corps will develop and publish special military standards, rules, or regulations prescribing appropriate safety and occupational health measures. Such special military-unique safety standards must be approved by the Commandant of the Marine Corps (Safety Division) (CMC (SD)). When approved, military-unique standards will meet the regulatory requirements of reference (a).

         (c) Embed risk management processes in planning for training and operations. Instill the requisite five step Operational Risk Management (ORM) skills in all personnel in order to enhance professional competence and improve force preservation. Risk management is a leadership responsibility that balances training and operational requirements with known risks and the mission at hand. Commanders positively influence safe behavior by setting the example and holding their Marines accountable for that behavior and performance.

         (d) Ensure safety personnel at all levels are fully qualified, per this Order. Safety Officers and Managers shall be assigned in writing and have direct access to the commander for all safety matters. All military personnel assigned safety responsibilities should keep those responsibilities for at least one year after such assignment.

         (e) Use inspection programs to evaluate all commands to ensure full implementation of the Marine Corps Safety Program and that all workplaces are free from recognized hazards.

   b. Subordinate Element Missions

      (1) Assistant Commandant of the Marine Corps (ACMC). The ACMC is the designated agency safety and health official for the Marine Corps and shall be listed on all posted DoD Safety Program DD Forms 2272. ACMC establishes safety policies and chairs the Marine Corps Executive Force Preservation Board (EFPB).

(2) <u>Director, Safety Division (Dir SD)</u>. The Dir SD is the designated Service safety chief and provides direct support to the ACMC in establishing safety policies and objectives, developing procedures, preparing and implementing directives, and administering, coordinating, and managing the Marine Corps Safety Program. Specifically, the Dir SD shall:

(a) Serve as the HQMC advocate for all safety programs: Aviation, Ground, Safety and Occupational Health (SOH), industrial hygiene, ergonomics, traffic safety (personal, commercial, and tactical), recreation, radiation (ionizing and non-ionizing), on- and off-duty safety programs, per references (d) and (e). Under the direction of the ACMC and the EFPB, and in conjunction with the Marine Forces (MARFORs) and Marine Corps installations, review all current safety initiatives and identify new programs for inclusion in the Program Objective Memorandum (POM) budgeting cycle.

(b) Establish policy and direction for the Marine Corps Safety Program in coordination with the EFPB, Deputy Commandants, Commanders, and other DoD, government, and non-government agencies, as appropriate.

(c) Oversee the Marine Corps Safety Program policy in the following areas: Aviation, Ground, SOH, industrial hygiene, ergonomics, motor vehicles (personal, commercial, and tactical), recreation, ionizing and non-ionizing radiation, explosives, ranges, on- and off-duty, per references (d) and (e).

(d) Review Marine Corps Orders sponsored by other Marine Corps agencies to ensure Marine Corps Safety Program requirements are addressed.

(e) Exercise the oversight responsibility identified in subparagraph 4b(2)(c) above by conducting Command Safety Assessments (CSA) to assess the status of command safety programs every three years. CSAs will be conducted at Marine Forces Command (MARFORCOM), Marine Forces Pacific (MARFORPAC), Marine Forces Special Operations Command (MARSOC), Marine Forces Reserves (MARFORRES), Marine Corps Combat Development Command (MCCDC), Marine Corps Recruiting Command (MCRC), Marine Corps Logistics Command (MARCORLOGCOM), Marine Corps Installations East (MCI-East), Marine Corps Installations West (MCI-West), Marine Corps Bases Japan, Marine Expeditionary Forces (MEFs), selected subordinate commands, and all installations. Report all findings to the respective commanders and provide trends and significant safety issues to ACMC.

(f) Analyze mishap data to identify causal factors and recommend policy for preventing mishap recurrence. Provide trends or significant safety issues to ACMC, the Deputy Commandant for Aviation and the Commander, Naval Safety Center (COMNAVSAFECEN). Sources of mishap data include but are not limited to personal casualty reports, the DoD Lost Workday Rate Top 40, Department of Labor web site for the President's Protecting Our Workers and Ensuring Reemployment (POWER) initiative performance, Web Enabled Safety System (WESS), and Warrior Preservation Status Report (WPSR) as well as appropriate Naval Aviation Safety Investigation Reports. Report Control Symbol MC-5100-05 is assigned to this reporting requirement.

(g) Serve as the single point of contact with external agencies for all Marine Corps Safety Program elements. Ensure the Marine Corps is represented on all DoD and Department of the Navy (DON) safety policy formulation groups, including the Defense Safety Oversight Council (DSOC), the DSOC Integration Group, the Joint Services Safety Council, and the DoD Safety & Occupational Health Committee.

(h) Maintain liaison and coordination with COMNAVSAFECEN for the support of Marine Corps safety programs.

(i) Assist MCCDC and Training and Education Command (TECOM) in development of safety training curricula to meet the needs of the Marine Corps.

(j) Develop safety award criteria, collect nominations, select award recipients, and publicize appropriately.

(k) Provide subject matter experts (SME) to support other Marine Corps agencies in the management of risk, eliminating unnecessary risk, and minimizing inherent risk, thereby directly contributing to force preservation and operational effectiveness and readiness.

(l) Maintain liaison and coordination with DoD, the Assistant Secretary of the Navy (Energy, Installations and Environment) (ASN EI&E), Bureau of Medicine and Surgery (BUMED) and CMC Health Services (HS) for the support of Marine Corps occupational health and industrial hygiene programs.

(m) Manage Marine Climate Assessment Survey System (GCASS) via the chain of command to the Division/Logistics Group/Aircraft Wing level. Report Control Symbol MC-5100-07 is assigned to this reporting requirement.

(n) Develop and implement Marine Corps policies regarding the Radiation Safety Program.

(o) Direct the management of all Naval Radioactive Materials Permits (NRMP) issued to Marine Corps commands. Conduct an assessment every two years of all Marine Corps NRMP and X-ray radiography programs.

(p) Ensure the publication and dissemination of information on the Marine Corps Safety Program. Collaborate with Headquarters Marine Corps Public Affairs Division to stimulate interest in safety through electronic and print media. Communicate safety success stories, share hazard awareness and near-miss lessons learned.

(q) Employ social media of all kinds to transmit the safety message.

(r) Employ new technologies to ensure safety programs operate and resources are used efficiently and effectively to achieve desired outcomes.

(3) Deputy Commandant for Aviation. Manage risk across the spectrum of Marine Corps aviation operations and related operations by advocating and providing direction for the Naval Aviation Safety Program, the Naval Air Training and Operating Procedures Standardization (NATOPS) programs for the Marine Corps, as well as the Marine Corps Aviation Training System (ATS).

(4) Deputy Commandant for Installation and Logistics. Implement those elements of the Marine Corps Safety Program concerning fire protection

and emergency services, radiation, hazardous materials, pollution prevention, property disposal, and hazardous waste.

(5) Deputy Commandant for Plans, Policies, and Operations. Act as the point of contact for firearms safety in areas of law enforcement (military police, guard forces, anti-terrorism/force protection, etc.), and motor vehicle safety as it relates to law enforcement. Coordinate with CMC (SD) staff at the Naval Safety Center(NAVSAFECEN) (Code 40), Norfolk VA for review of all parachuting mishap information and conduct of biannual parachute safety inspections.

(6) Deputy Commandant for Manpower and Reserve Affairs

(a) Collect and analyze suicide data and provide analyses as required by higher headquarters.

(b) Provide monthly trend analysis to CMC SD on civilian lost production days, lost workday rates, lost time case rates, suicides, and suicide attempts.

(c) Ensure Injury Compensation Program Administrators (ICPA) support Marine Corps safety officers and managers to locally manage lost production days.

(7) Deputy Commandant for Programs and Resources. Ensure all commands are appropriately funded for implementation of the Marine Corps Safety Program.

(8) Commanding General, Training and Education Command

(a) Incorporate Safety and Occupational Health (SOH) and risk management into the curricula of all military and civilian training and education.

(b) Research, develop, publish, and disseminate curricula for all safety professional development courses, e.g., Ground Safety for Marines and Operational Risk Management.

(c) Develop, implement, and provide institutional oversight for the Marine Corps Range Safety Program to include ground, aviation, and LASER training on Operational Ranges.

$\underline{1}$. Develop and publish appropriate range safety guidance. Develop and publish Training and Education Command (TECOM) Safety of Use Memoranda (SOUM) for Marine Corps unique weapons, munitions, and training systems per MARADMIN 612/02.

$\underline{2}$. Fund the Marine Corps Range Safety Program per Marine Corps Requirements Oversight Council Decision Memorandum 57-2005.

$\underline{3}$. Represent the Marine Corps on the North Atlantic Treaty Organization (NATO) Range Safety Working Group (NRSWG), International Range Safety Advisory Group (IRSAG) and various DoD-level groups, boards, committees, or other organizations that address safety within ranges and training areas.

4. Ensure new weapons, ammunition, LASERs and training systems have the appropriate safety approvals/certifications, and range safety technical data prior to fielding and use on Operational Ranges.

5. Provide SMEs to support Marine Corps commands on Safety Investigation Boards (SIB) investigating mishaps on Marine Corps ranges and training areas.

(d) Develop and implement a driver improvement training course for all military personnel, targeted as high-risk drivers.

(9) Commander, Marine Corps Systems Command

(a) Incorporate SOH and risk management into the materiel life cycle management process.

(b) Ensure appropriate weapons systems, as well as new and modified munitions, are reviewed by the Weapon Systems Explosives Safety Review Board, LASER Safety Review Board, Navy Radiation Safety Committee, and Lithium Battery Review Board during the systems acquisition process.

(c) Establish policy for suspending operations of Marine Corps ground equipment and weapons systems due to unsafe conditions, including issuance of appropriate instructions and safety of use alerts.

(d) Ensure consideration of SOH features in the design, purchase, or procurement of all items over which the command exercises acquisition authority.

(e) Implement the Marine Corps Environmental and Explosives Safety Program and represent the Marine Corps on the DoD Explosives Safety Board and other DoD-level groups, boards, committee, or other organizations that address explosives.

(f) Provide SMEs for SIBs involving material related failures of Marine Corps owned ground equipment and/or explosives, when requested by the senior board member via the controlling command.

(g) Serve as the Marine Corps point of contact with external agencies for all systems safety and acquisition elements. Ensure the Marine Corps is represented on all DoD and DON safety policy formulation groups, including, e.g., the Defense Safety Oversight Council (DSOC) and all pertinent task forces and working groups.

(10) Inspector General of the U.S. Marine Corps. Review implementation of the Marine Corps Safety Program during command inspections.

(11) Director, Health Services

(a) Provide occupational health (industrial hygiene, occupational audiology, and occupational medical surveillance) and public health (preventive medicine, field and camp sanitation) consultative support and coordination with BUMED, as needed.

(b) Provide consultative support and coordination with DC M&RA on all matters pertaining to suicide prevention.

(12) <u>Installation Commanders (Bases and Stations)</u>

(a) Ensure the resourcing and management of an installation-wide safety and occupational health program, per enclosure (1), Chapter 1 of this Order, including execution of the installation's core safety services.

(b) Conduct and document an annual self-assessment of core safety services to ensure full implementation. Maintain documented self assessments for three years for review by higher authorities.

(c) Installation commanders or deputies shall chair quarterly Drive Safe Councils, with the installation safety office providing support and maintaining minutes.

(d) Require tenant organizations to comply with all applicable safety standards.

(e) Ensure safety oversight of contractor operations, via the local contracting officer.

(f) Contracts shall require contractors to comply with requirements of this Order.

(g) Contractors shall bring to the attention of the command, through established procedures and without fear of reprisals, the existence of any unsafe or unhealthful operation or work condition.

(13) <u>Commanders shall</u>:

(a) Establish a safety program that meets requirements of this Order, including a published command safety policy and mission statement.

(b) Assign, in writing, the responsibility for execution of the safety program to the deputy commander or executive officer (XO).

(c) Conduct safety climate surveys using the GCASS in compliance with chapter 2 of enclosure (1). Report Control Symbol MC-5100-07 is assigned to this reporting requirement.

(d) Comply with chapter (3) of enclosure (1) for commands required to maintain a command aviation safety program.

(e) Ensure operational pauses and/or Back In the Saddle (BITS) Operational Pauses are held at least semiannually following an extended holiday period or post-deployment.

(f) Ensure all serious mishaps (Class A and B) and non-combat deaths other than due to morbidity are briefed to the first general officer in the chain of command using the 8-Day Brief template provided on the CMC SD website. This includes deaths due to suicide and criminal activity. No later than the 8th day following the mishap or other death, the first general officer shall provide this brief to the ACMC with a copy to the chain of command, CMC SD, and, for aviation mishaps, DC AVN. For suicides, the brief will also be copied to the Behavioral Health Affairs Officer, Manpower and Reserve Affairs. This brief shall provide the circumstances surrounding the mishap and the necessary steps to prevent a recurrence. The 8-Day Brief is not required for Reserve Marines in a non-drilling status or Individual Ready Reserve Marines.

(g) Deliver a Death Brief for all non-combat deaths other than due to morbidity to the first General Officer in the chain of command. Commanding generals need only receive the Death Brief by exception but are responsible for gleaning and distributing those lessons learned that have applicability to the Marine Corps. SD will assist with distribution as required. Death Briefs are not typically briefed to ACMC or SD, but a copy of the final brief will be provided electronically to each for information only. The Death Brief will contain greater detail and is presented after all facts surrounding the fatality are known. Death Brief examples are provided on the CMC (SD) web site and may be tailored, as necessary, by the receiving general officer. The Death Brief is not required to be submitted for Reserve Marines in a non-drilling status or Individual Ready Reserve Marines.

(h) Establish a safety office, as special staff to the commander, led by a fully qualified safety officer or civilian manager appointed in writing, to serve as the command's senior technical advisor for SOH matters and to execute the following:

<u>1</u>. Support the deputy commander or XO in the execution of the command's safety program per this Order.

<u>2</u>. Identify, establish, and appropriately train staff for required safety billets, (e.g., safety officer or civilian manager, safety specialists and safety representatives).

<u>3</u>. Provide technical advice, direction, and guidance on safety matters to subordinate elements.

<u>4</u>. Interpret safety standards and regulations and develop, or participate in development of new or revised command-level standards, when appropriate.

<u>5</u>. Use the U.S. Marine Corps Inspector General's Automated Inspection and Reporting System Functional Areas 130 (non-aviation), 870, and 875 (aviation) checklists or CMC SD CSA checklist to conduct and document an annual self-assessment of the command safety program.

<u>6</u>. Ensure the U.S. Marine Corps safety programs are implemented at all subordinate commands and installations.

<u>7</u>. Employ new technologies and ensure safety programs operate and resources are used efficiently and effectively to achieve desired objectives as required.

<u>8</u>. Serve as the command representative on safety councils, committees, and working groups established by higher authority.

<u>9</u>. Analyze command mishaps and occupational illnesses, e.g., hearing loss, and provide quarterly trend analysis to the commander.

10. Collect, analyze, and forward via the chain of command data for the annual U.S. Marine Corps Report to Department of Labor on Occupational Safety and Health. Information shall be provided to CMC SD by 15 November each year.

11. Request investigation assistance from Commander MARCORSYSCOM for all Class A and B mishaps involving Marine Corps-owned ground equipment, when necessary.

12. Ensure industrial hygiene reports are reviewed and recommendations incorporated into command hazard tracking system (hazard abatement logs) for documented follow-up actions.

(i) Ensure the safety office personnel maintain sufficient knowledge, authority, and responsibility to resource and execute SOH programs.

(j) Ensure the publication and dissemination of information on the command's safety program. Collaborate with public affairs office to stimulate interest in safety through electronic and print media. Communicate safety success stories, share hazard awareness and near-miss lessons learned.

(k) Satisfy the requirements of the Marine Corps Safety Program and submit a WPSR, per enclosure (1), Chapter 4. Aviation commands must additionally report satisfaction of aviation specific requirements via the ORM Status Report per enclosure (1) Chapter 3. Report Control Symbol MC-5100-05 is assigned to this reporting requirement.

(l) Safety officers, managers, or directors shall not be assigned to Judge Advocate General (JAG) or other non-safety mishap investigations or other safety-related incident.

(14) <u>Military and DoD civilian personnel of the Marine Corps shall</u>:

(a) Comply with the requirements of the Marine Corps Safety Program.

(b) Bring to the attention of the command through established procedures the existence of any unsafe or unhealthful operation or working condition.

(c) Military personnel shall report both on- and off-duty mishaps and near misses (a near miss is an unplanned event that did not result in injury, illness, or damage - but had the potential to do so) to their supervisor. DoD civilian personnel shall report all on-duty mishaps and near misses to their supervisors.

(d) All supervisors, including all E4 and higher Marines and Sailors, as well as civilian supervisors identified by position description, shall report via their chain of command all on- and off-duty mishaps and near misses to their respective command safety office.

c. Coordinating Instructions

(1) Host-Tenant Relationships. Installation commanders are responsible for the overall health and safety of all personnel aboard the installation, particularly as specified below.

(a) A Memorandum of Understanding (MOU), Memorandum of Agreement (MOA), or Inter-Service Support Agreement (ISSA) shall specify safety support in host-tenant relationships. Safety support will not be reimbursable unless the services required by the tenant are outside the scope of the host's safety service capability.

(b) Tenant commands aboard Marine Corps installations shall adhere to the host installation's safety standards. Marine Corps tenants of other DoD installations shall adhere to the host's safety standards. Where tenant commands have safety standards that meet or exceed the host command's requirements, tenant commands shall adhere to the more stringent standards.

(c) Installation safety offices shall provide the core safety services described in enclosure (1), Chapter 1 to all personnel on the installation unless precluded by an ISSA, MOU or MOA.

(2) Commander, Naval Safety Center (COMNAVSAFECEN). By MOA with CMC (SD), COMNAVSAFECEN supports the Marine Corps Safety Program in the following manner:

(a) Provides mishap report collection, data and statistical analysis, technical assistance, safety surveys, publications support, culture workshops, conducts independent safety investigations of major mishaps, and safety program consultations.

(b) Supports Marine Corps commanders with mishap investigation advisors for Class A mishaps.

(c) Upon request, provides a mishap investigation advisor to assist commanders with any safety investigation.

(3) Military Medical Treatment Facility (MTF) Support

(a) BUMED provides to support CMC in all aspects of occupational health, including industrial hygiene, occupational and environmental medicine, and occupational audiology.

(b) All Marine Corps commands will use the local MTF for all occupational health support.

(c) Marine Corps commanders shall ensure Marines and DoD civilian personnel receive their occupational health services. Where such support is not available, commanders shall ensure that occupational health services acquired.

5. Administration and Logistics

a. Commanders shall ensure adequate staff and budgets are provided to implement a comprehensive safety program that meets the requirements of this Order and other applicable orders.

b. Commanders shall integrate risk management strategies into appropriate planning, orders, training and indoctrination programs, technical and tactical publications, checklists, and standard operating procedures.

c. Records created as a result of this directive shall include records management requirements to ensure the proper maintenance and use of records, regardless of format or medium, to promote accessibility and authorized retention per the approved records schedule.

6. Command and Signal

a. Command. This Order is applicable to the Marine Corps Total Force. It is applicable to all active duty Marines on or off duty, as well as reserve Marines and DoD civilian personnel on duty. This Order extends to military family members and all other civilian personnel, including contractors while on Marine Corps installations, participants in any Marine Corps sponsored events, operations, or training, and applies to all Marine Corps facilities, equipment, and materiel.

b. Signal. This Order is effective the date signed.

JOSEPH F. DUNFORD, JR.
Assistant Commandant
of the Marine Corps

DISTRIBUTION: PCN 10207241200

Copy to: 7000260/8145005 (2)
          7000099, 114/8145001 (1)

LOCATOR SHEET

Subj: MARINE CORPS SAFETY PROGRAM

Location: _____
          (Indicate the location(s) of copy(ies) of this Order.)

RECORD OF CHANGES

Log completed change action as indicated.

Change Number	Date of Change	Date Entered	Signature of Person Change

TABLE OF CONTENTS

IDENTIFICATION	TITLE	PAGE
Chapter 1	Marine Corps Bases and Stations Core Safety Services	1-1
1.	Support Military Operations and Training	1-1
2.	Traffic Safety	1-1
3.	Safety Promotional Material	1-2
4.	Resource, Manage and Provide Installation-Wide Safety	1-2
5.	Safety Inspections	1-2
6.	Mishap Investigations	1-3
7.	Personal Protective Equipment (PPE)	1-3
8.	Safety Training	1-3
9.	Safety Consultation	1-4
10.	Coordination of Occupational Health Services	1-4
Chapter 2	Marine Corps Ground Safety Requirements	2-1
1.	Applicability	2-1
2.	Coordination of Safety Services	2-1
3.	Elements of Ground Safety Program	2-1
4.	Ground Safety Officer	2-2
5.	Mishap Investigations and Reporting	2-3
6.	Concept of Privilege in Safety Investigations	2-4
Chapter 3	Marine Corps Aviation Safety Requirements	3-1
1.	Aviation Activities	3-1
2.	Commanding Officer	3-1
3.	Department of Safety and Standardization (DOSS)	3-1
4.	Mishap Reporting	3-4
5.	Recurring Requirements	3-5
Figure 3-1	Operational Risk Management Status Report	3-12
Chapter 4	Warrior Preservation Status Report (WPSR) Instructions	4-1
1.	WPSR Purpose	4-1
2.	Reporting Requirements	4-1
3.	WPSR Template Location	4-1
4.	WPSR Business Rules	4-1
5.	Scoring	4-1
Figure 4-1	WPSR criteria and instructions	4-2
Chapter 5	Operational Risk Management (ORM)	5-1
1.	ORM Process	5-1
2.	ORM Principles	5-1
3.	5-Setp ORM Process	5-1
4.	ORM Details	5-2

Chapter 1

Marine Corps Bases and Stations Core Safety Services

As a component of the "fifth element" of the Marine Air Ground Task Force (MAGTF) and in support of the Marine Corps' operating forces: All Marine Corps installation safety offices shall be resourced to provide these core safety services on a non-reimbursable basis to all organizations physically located on the installation. The following core safety services shall be provided by all Marine Corps installations:

1. <u>Support Military Operations and Training</u>. Provide qualified safety specialists for operational training, pre-deployment and deployment operations to ensure safety expertise, guidance, and assistance is available to identify hazards, assess risk, and develop and implement control measures to mitigate hazards. DON military and civilian safety specialists completing the U.S. Army's Career Program-12 intern course may be designated as Tactical Safety Specialists (TSS) to specifically support military operations and training. TSSs shall provide all safety programs described in paragraphs 2-10 of this chapter to assigned commands.

2. <u>Traffic Safety</u>. Develop, implement, and supervise a complete traffic safety program. Installation commanders, via the installation Safety Manager, shall:

   a. Ensure a written traffic safety program is established that incorporates all commands and other activities within the boundaries of their respective areas. The installation safety manager shall appoint a traffic safety program specialist within the installation safety office. Installation commanders or deputies shall chair quarterly Drive Safe Councils, with the installation safety office providing support and maintaining minutes. Commanders of battalions, squadrons, and tenant activities shall establish a written traffic safety program that supports and complements the program established by the host installation. The installation safety office shall coordinate or provide documented driver's awareness training to all military personnel under the age of 26.

   b. Provide the full range of motorcycle rider safety courses designed to enable Marines, Sailors, DoD civilian personnel, and family members the opportunity to earn state issued motorcycle endorsements and to learn the skills necessary to ride safely. Courses will include, but are not limited to: Basic Rider Course, Military Sportbike Riders Course, Experienced Riders Course, and other courses accepted by CMC (SD).

   c. Oversee Emergency Vehicle Operator Courses. Marines and DoD civilian personnel assigned to drive DoD police vehicles, ambulances, fire trucks, crash and rescue vehicles, or other response vehicles equipped with lights and siren are required to attend an emergency vehicle operator course.

   d. Provide remedial driver training courses. The purposes of remedial classes are to foster a positive change in behavior while driving. The National Safety Council's "Alive at 25" and "The Attitudinal Dynamic of Driving" are two examples of excellent courses to provide to personnel identified as at risk for automobile mishap or collision.

   e. Provide traffic mishap trend analysis and traffic safety education as a continual and ongoing process. The results of any traffic analysis or survey shall be shared installation wide for use at safety stand-down events, briefings, meetings, and other traffic safety events.

3. <u>Safety Promotional Material</u>. Ensure the safety office maintains a comprehensive public information program, which includes posters, booklets, handouts, promotional giveaway items (pencils, coins, mugs, magnets, rulers, etc), and other means to promote safety programs and themes aboard the base. Literature includes fire prevention, family safety, child care, Recreational and Off-Duty Safety (RODS), traffic safety, and other subjects important to the community.

4. <u>Resource, Manage and Provide Installation-Wide Safety</u>. Ensure a comprehensive, effective, and continuous installation-wide safety program is resourced and managed, through the application of recognized safety and occupational health principles, for all Marine Corps activities, units, and personnel aboard the installation.

5. <u>Safety Inspections</u>. Qualified safety and occupational health specialists shall conduct and document safety inspections of all installation and tenant work centers, buildings, training facilities, and ranges at least annually and provide recommended corrective actions. Inspections shall include a review of applicable safety and occupational health programs. All child development centers, children, youth, and teen programs, and family home child care facilities shall be inspected quarterly. Formal MOA may permit a qualified GS 0018 safety specialist of a tenant organization the responsibility for evaluating command safety programs.

    a. Safety hazards having the greatest risk to life or property damage, operations experiencing repeated mishaps, or require additional monitoring, shall be inspected more frequently or at least every six months. Maintain a log of identified hazards, abatement actions and date corrected.

    b. Execute all occupational safety and health programs required by reference (f).

    c. A certified Explosives Safety Officer (ESO) shall manage the installation's explosives safety program under the oversight of the installation safety manager.

    d. Investigate and document all reports of unsafe or unhealthful work conditions, including occupational health hazards identified in an industrial hygiene survey on the installation. Maintain a log of identified safety and occupational health hazards, interim abatement actions, and date corrected.

    e. Accompany all external federal and/or state safety and occupational health inspectors on SOH inspections. Report such inspections via the chain of command to CMC (SD) within 48 hours of inspection commencement. Provide follow up reports via the chain of command detailing results of the inspection and documenting planned or completed abatement actions for hazards or deficiencies identified, as soon as they are available.

    f. Ensure installation safety officers and managers collaborate with Injury Compensation Program Administrators (ICPA) to reduce DoD civilian personnel lost work time due to injury.

6. <u>Mishap Investigations</u>. Mishap and near mishap investigation and reporting are critical to the success of the safety program. Upon request

from a tenant command, installation safety managers shall provide support to investigating commanders to ensure mishap investigations are conducted.

   a.   Ensure all installation mishaps and near misses are investigated by qualified personnel.

   b.   Investigations shall commence as soon as possible after the mishap occurs and shall proceed concurrently with other command investigations that may be ongoing, e.g., legal investigations. If evidence of criminal activity is causal to the mishap is discovered, the safety investigator should suspend the investigation, preserve the evidence, and immediately notify the safety investigation convening authority, the appropriate military criminal investigative organization, and the safety investigation convening authority's staff judge advocate. The safety investigation convening authority will determine whether, or not, the mishap investigation will proceed after consultation with the staff judge advocate.

   c.   Provide technical assistance in the preparation of all required 8-day reports and Death Briefs.

7.   Personal Protective Equipment (PPE). During safety inspections and surveys, document PPE (e.g. head, sight, hearing, respiratory and foot protection) requirements and compliance. Ensure appropriate PPE training and fit testing is conducted, and that PPE is available, used, and maintained.

8.   Safety Training. The installation safety manager shall provide safety training for all personnel on the installation, including tenant units. Commanders shall ensure attendance at all safety and ORM training. This training shall be provided by qualified safety specialists.

   a.   Per reference (b), all supervisory personnel are required to receive specialized safety training. Specifically, supervisor safety training shall include an overview of the command safety program, mishap investigation and reporting, responsibility to train their subordinates, identify operations and personnel at risk to occupational health hazards identified by industrial hygiene and safety surveys, development and implementation of Job Hazard Analyses (JHA), and all items specified by reference (b).

   b.   All Marines, Sailors, and DoD civilian personnel shall attend documented annual safety training appropriate for their job, including a review of all applicable Job Hazard Analysis.

   c.   Provide or coordinate documented training and technical assistance for LASER, radiation, radio frequency radiation safety programs, and all SOH training.

9.   Safety Consultation. Upon request, the installation safety office will provide professional support for special events and exercises for all organizations on the installation. Ensure the application of risk management principles for new construction, renovation projects, and service contracts.

10.   Coordination of Occupational Health Services

   a.   Commanders shall ensure documented occupational health and industrial hygiene services are received from the local MTF. Safety, occupational health, and industrial hygiene personnel should collaborate in the analysis of injury, illness, work center inspection trends, and other findings to brief command safety council meetings. Occupational health services may include, but not limited to, support as appropriate for the Command's Hearing Conservation, Respiratory Protection, Bloodborne Pathogens, Asbestos Exposure, and Lead Exposure Programs.

b. In general, BUMED occupational health and industrial hygiene services are not provided to contract employees working on Marine Corps installations. The Occupational Safety and Health Act requires contractors to ensure the SOH of their employees.

c. Vision screening (e.g., visual acuity, visual fields, and color vision) is required to evaluate whether employees (or employee applicants) meet essential job elements.

d. The installation safety office shall consult with supply officers and the MTF to determine the most suitable procurement procedures when prescription protective eyewear is required. It is a civilian employee's responsibility to obtain an eye refraction exam and secure an accompanying prescription for safety glasses (comprehensive vision examinations are a personal health responsibility and are strongly recommended in conjunction with an eye refraction examination). Installation commanding officers shall establish procedures for obtaining prescription safety eyewear through contracts, reimbursement, MTF, or other methods. Such procedures shall comply with provisions of master labor agreements covered under 5 USC Chapter 71, other provisions of law providing for collective bargaining agreements and procedures, and any agreements entered into under such provisions.

e. Medical surveillance requirements shall be provided by the MTF. When these services are provided, all medical forms and evaluations must be documented according to the BUMED Manual of Medical Department.

Chapter 2

Marine Corps Ground Safety Requirements

1. **Applicability**. While the size of a command may impact a commander's ability to comply with some provisions of this chapter, all commanders are charged with employing their available manpower and resources to meet the intent of this chapter to the maximum extent possible. This chapter applies to aviation commands, squadrons and stations as well as chapter 3 of this Order.

2. **Coordination of Safety Services**. Core Safety Services (CSS) outlined in Chapter 1 shall be provided on a nonreimbursable basis by the base or station safety office. Commanders shall ensure their personnel have access to and use the CSS.

   (a) Fire prevention services are provided by the local fire prevention office.

   (b) TSSs are highly trained safety professionals who possess experience in MAGTF operations. Those TSS not already assigned to the operating forces are available to deploy in support of field training and overseas contingency operations upon request via the chain of command.

   (c) Coordinate appropriate occupational health services via the chain of command from the nearest MTF. Occupational health services may include, but are not limited to support as appropriate for the unit's industrial hygiene, medical surveillance, hearing conservation, respiratory protection, bloodborne pathogens, asbestos exposure, and lead exposure programs. Such support requires worksite visits, consultation and attendance to MTF for treatment.

3. **Elements of Ground Safety Program**. To develop and maintain a comprehensive ground safety program, unit commanders shall:

   a. Publish a safety policy within 30 days of assuming command.

   b. O5 and O6 level commanders will appoint a ground safety officer or manager in writing, as a special staff officer with direct access to the commander for safety matters. The ground safety officer or manager shall have a staff to support the mission with, as a minimum, a staff noncommissioned officer (SNCO) with a secondary Military Occupational Specialty (MOS) 8012 (Ground Safety Officer).

   c. Appoint in writing an NCO or civilian as shop/section safety representatives.

   d. Ensure personnel receive adequate safety training. Specifically:

   (1) Ground safety officer or manager and SNCO personnel shall attend the Ground Safety for Marines (GSM) course within 90 days of appointment. Keeping trained ground safety officer or manager and SNCO in safety billets at least one year allows commands to recoup costs and improve safety programs.

   (2) Supervisors shall attend initial and annual safety awareness training provided per reference (b) by the command safety office.

(3) Other safety training may be necessary based on the results of safety and industrial hygiene surveys or specific MOS or billet requirements. Such training shall be coordinated via the chain of command.

e. Ensure risk management principles are embedded in the culture of the command and all Marines and Sailors attend initial and annual Operational Risk Management (ORM) training.

f. Conduct operational pauses, e.g. BITS pauses, at least semiannually. Operational pauses and safety stand-downs are synonymous and provide a break from operations to conduct safety training, review procedures, and assess the command's safety posture. To facilitate the best use of time, operational pauses should be planned well in advance and integrated into training plans.

g. Unit commanders shall ensure the health of the command safety program and the command climate. Safety climate surveys are a valuable tool for assessing each. Conduct safety climate surveys using the GCASS (RCS MC-5100-07) in compliance with the following instructions. Report Control Symbol MC-5100-07 is assigned to this reporting requirement.

(1) Commanders of Marine Forces Command, Marine Forces Pacific, Marine Forces Reserves, Marine Forces Special Operations Command, Marine Corps Combat Development Command, Marine Corps Logistics Command, Marine Corps Systems Command, Marine Corps Recruiting Command, Marine Expeditionary Forces, all Marine Aircraft Wings (MAWs), all Marine Logistics Groups, and all Divisions conduct the higher headquarters survey within 90 days of assuming command and annually thereafter.

(2) O5 and O6-level commanders not designated to conduct aviation specific surveys per Chapter 3 of this Order shall conduct a Ground Climate Assessment Survey to assess the command climate within 90 days of change of command (to establish a baseline for the new commander) and annually, thereafter.

(3) Aviation commanding officers have the discretion and are encouraged to access, via the GCASS website, a set of ground safety climate surveys to assess the posture of a commander's ground safety programs. Marine squadrons shall access all ground safety climate surveys specifically on the GCASS website. Do not access ground safety climate surveys via the "Aviation Commands Only" icon.

(4) All commanding officers have the individual discretion and are encouraged to use other surveys available through the GCASS as they deem beneficial.

(4) GCASS can be accessed through the CMC SD web site, http://www.marines.mil/unit/safety/Pages/welcome.aspx. Instructions for administering the surveys may be found on the website under the "Survey Information" menu item along the left side of the web page.

4. Ground Safety Officer (GSO). The command ground safety officer or manager shall ensure the following ground safety components are accomplished.

a. Safety Meetings. At least quarterly, the CO or XO shall conduct command safety and safe driving councils, advising unit leaders of safety challenges, current trends, hazard corrective actions taken or required, local traffic safety issues, on- and off-duty mishaps, and other force preservation and readiness issues. Prepare and maintain file copies of the minutes of these meetings for three years. Unit commanders or a designated representative should also participate in installation safety council meetings.

b. <u>Safety Inspections</u>. Conduct quarterly safety inspections of all command facilities, processes, and equipment. Document the results and forward an executive summary of inspection results to the commander. These inspections are intended to augment the annual safety inspection conducted by fully qualified safety and occupational health specialists.

c. <u>Hazard Abatement</u>. Commanders shall ensure identified safety hazards are immediately corrected or mitigated with interim fixes and tracked in a hazard abatement log until corrected. Retain the hazard abatement logs for three years.

d. <u>Turnover Binders</u>. Ensure unit and shop/workcenter or sections maintain appropriate safety turnover binders with the following:

(1) Appointment letters.

(2) Safety Standard Operating Procedures.

(3) Inventory of known hazards (include hazardous noise sources and processes, list of PPE and medical surveillance required per industrial hygiene survey).

(4) Hazard abatement log of uncorrected hazards with interim controls (include date hazard identified, date of interim control and date of corrected hazard).

(5) Maintain an inventory of unit facilities by building number and a map of their location. Ensure numbers of assigned civilian and military personnel are readily available.

(6) By-name list of personnel who require medical surveillance (hearing test, respirator physicals, vehicle operator's examinations, etc). The list shall include the expiration dates of training and certifications and be provided to the responsible workplace supervisors.

(7) Ensure supervisory annual safety training is documented in official training records. Include training and expiration dates. Provide expiration information to the responsible supervisor.

e. <u>Anonymous Safety Reporting</u>. Establish procedures and train all personnel on the procedures for reporting unsafe or unhealthful working conditions via NAVMC 11401 or ANYMOUSE (RCS MC-5100-06) forms.

5. <u>Mishap Investigations and Reporting</u>.

a. Investigate all mishaps to determine causes, classification, and reporting requirements.

b. Convene a SIB, when required.

c. Conduct trend analysis of unit mishaps and identified hazards in order to develop mitigation and prevention strategies.

d. Maintain records of all unit mishaps for 5 years.

e. Submit mishap reports via WESS.

f. Ensure corrective actions identified through a mishap investigation are completed in a timely manner.

g. Submit an Annual Summary of Marine Corps Work-Related Injuries and Illnesses and the OSHA 300A via the chain of command and, as appropriate, copy the host installation safety office.

6. <u>Concept of Privilege in Safety Investigations</u>

a. Privilege encourages individuals involved in the safety investigation process to provide complete, open, and forthright information, opinions, causes, and recommendations about a mishap.

b. Determining the privileged elements of a safety investigation is a subjective process. The following items are generally considered privileged information.

(1) <u>Evidence</u>. Photographs, drawings, maps, charts, videos, etc., a safety investigator stages or annotates are privileged. Information directly calculated by a safety investigator or developed at the specific request of the safety investigator is privileged when that information would reveal the process leading to the development of conclusions, causes, and recommendations.

(2) <u>Witness Statements</u>. Witness statements to a SIB shall not be provided to any activity. Once the witness makes a statement to the SIB, the contents of the statement become part of the SIB's evidence. Safety investigators may only grant promises of confidentiality to witnesses in investigations of flight related accidents or friendly fire mishaps. Only Secretaries of the Military Departments may authorize the granting of confidentiality to witnesses regarding accidents involving complex systems or military unique items, or military unique operations or exercises. Promises of confidentiality are not authorized for any other type of accident. Safety investigators are encouraged to avoid taking signed statements from witnesses, but rather should create summaries of interview from the notes made from such interviews. Safety investigators should avoid showing the witness interviewed the summary of interview or the investigator's notes from that interview in order to avoid discovery issues, if the incident results in a subsequent disciplinary proceeding.

(3) <u>Safety Investigation Reports</u>. The preparation of the safety investigation report requires the command safety investigator or SIB to analyze the information gathered which leads to the development of conclusions, causes, and recommendations. Therefore, those parts of the safety investigation report are privileged.

c. Further assistance and guidance for privileged information is available from the NAVSAFECEN.

Chapter 3

Marine Corps Aviation Safety Requirements

1. Aviation Activities. Reference (g) defines the overarching Naval
Aviation Safety Program. This order supplements reference (g) with
additional U.S. Marine Corps specific requirements.

2. Commanding Officer

    a. Commanding officers of flying squadrons, Marine Unmanned Aerial
Vehicle (VMU) squadrons, Marine Aviation Logistic Squadrons (MALS), and
Marine Aircraft Groups (MAGs) are required by paragraph 5a of this chapter to
submit a monthly ORM Status Report. Commanding officers shall review and
approve the release of the Command's ORM Status Report per this Order.

    b. Commanders of Marine Corps aviation organizations that are aircraft
reporting custodians shall complete the School of Aviation Safety (SAS)
Aviation Safety Command (ASC) course prior to or within 2 years preceding
assumption of command. This requirement is considered a minimal acceptable
requirement and is reported as such in the ORM Status Report detailed in this
chapter.

3. Department of Safety and Standardization Structure and Responsibilities.
All reporting custodian squadrons and permanent aviation detachments (such as
a Marine Transport Squadron 1 (VMR-1) Detachment (Det)), shall establish a
Department of Safety and Standardization (DOSS) as detailed below.

    a. Director of Safety and Standardization (DOSS)

        (1) Directly responsible to, and shall have direct access to the
commander on all safety and standardization matters.

        (2) Implement the commander's safety and standardization policies.
Supervise the aviation and ground mishap prevention programs in order to
identify and eliminate or control hazards.

        (3) Exercise staff cognizance over the Naval Air Training and
Operating Procedures Standardization (NATOPS), aviation safety, and ground
safety programs.

        (4) Be on a level with all other department heads.

        (5) Should not be assigned collateral duties or responsibilities
outside the DOSS.

        (6) Should be a graduate of the SAS ASC course or the SAS Aviation
Safety Officer (ASO) Course.

        (7) Shall ensure the following standing bodies are formed and meet as
required in reference (g) and this Order: Aviation Safety Council, Enlisted
Aviation Safety Committee, Standardization Board, Human Factors Council, and
Instrument Flight Board.

        (8) Shall compile and submit the monthly ORM Status Report to the
commander per this Order and assist the commander in monitoring and
accomplishing the minimum acceptable requirements reflected in the report.

(9) Shall support the XO in the execution of the unit safety program. Develop and implement procedures and processes which tie maintenance, operations, safety, and training towards a common goal of preventing mishaps and managing risk. Ensure safety programs operate and resources are used efficiently and effectively to achieve desired outcomes.

(10) Shall oversee and ensure aviation training is conducted to balance risk through smart training, awareness of risks present, and a clear understanding of the mission at hand.

(11) Shall not be assigned to other investigative duties.

b. <u>Aviation Safety Officer (ASO)</u>. Commanders should select their ASO with a weight matching that's given to the selection of the squadron's Weapons and Tactics Instructor or Quality Assurance Officer. Commanders should consider experience level, demonstrated judgment and maturity, as well as the officer's ability to work with and affect other departments within the squadron when selecting the officer with which to entrust the squadron's Aviation Safety Program and its contributing piece to the larger Marine Corps Aviation Safety Program. The requirement to have a school trained ASO is considered a minimum acceptable requirement and is reported on the ORM Status Report.

(1) <u>ASO Requirements</u>

(a) Shall be a graduate of the SAS ASO Course. Every effort should be made to assign an officer that has completed the ASO course within the previous four years.

(b) The ASO shall be a highly-qualified, winged aviator, of the rank of captain or major.

(c) ASOs shall possesses flight designations commensurate with their peer group, with the minimum being that of Section Leader. Exceptions for the Section Leader requirement are the qualification as a Transport Plane Commander for KC-130 pilots, 750 total flight hours for Naval Flight Officers, and Mission Commander for VMU ASOs.

(d) Exceptional candidates may be ready to serve as ASOs ahead of their peers and prior to meeting the enumerated requirements. Therefore, waivers to these minimum standards will be considered on a case-by-case basis. Waiver authority to deviate from these requirements resides with the Wing Commanding General or first general officer in the chain of command.

(2) <u>ASO Duties</u>

(a) Develop, implement, and execute a proactive Aviation Safety Program in order to identify and eliminate or control hazards.

(b) Advise and have direct access to the commander and the DSS on all matters pertaining to the organization's aviation safety program.

(c) Monitor flight and aircraft maintenance activities for compliance with appropriate directives and standardization.

(d) Assist the Quality Assurance Officer in monitoring quality assurance and collateral duty programs as outlined in the Naval Aviation Maintenance Program.

(e) Conduct pre-mishap plan drills and training annually. Ensure the pre-mishap plan is updated prior to any change of operating base/area. Pre-mishap training should focus on risk assessment, mishap prevention, and on-post mishap duties and responsibilities. This training shall include watch-stander roles and responsibilities during emergency situations to ensure they are trained and skilled in actions that may prevent emergency situations from becoming mishaps.

(f) Shall conduct sufficient training of the Aircraft Mishap Board (AMB) to ensure the squadron has a capability to activate a primary and alternate AMB if required.

(g) Should not be assigned collateral duties or responsibilities outside the DOSS.

c. NATOPS Officer

(1) Establish and maintain a dynamic and proactive standardization program per appropriate NATOPS flight manuals.

(2) Administer the NATOPS program.

(3) Conduct NATOPS jacket audits.

(4) Coordinate Unit NATOPS evaluation. The Unit NATOPS Evaluation is considered a minimum acceptable standard and is reported on the ORM Status Report.

d. Ground Safety Officer (GSO). Maintain a comprehensive ground safety program, including training requirements, as specified in Chapter 2 of this enclosure.

e. Enlisted NATOPS NCO/Aviation Safety Specialist. For organizations with enlisted aircrew assigned, the NATOPS NCO/Aviation Safety Specialist shall assist the NATOPS Officer and ASO in all matters pertaining to NATOPS and Aviation Safety programs, enlisted flight crew training, standardization, human factors council, and enlisted safety committees.

f. Flight Surgeon (FS) and Aeromedical Safety Officer (AMSO). Flight Surgeons and AMSOs are assigned throughout the Marine Corps chain of command. Most aeromedical specialists reside on the staff at MAWs, MAGs, and in the case of FSs, down to individual flying squadrons. Their primary duty is mishap prevention through an engaged and proactive presence ensuring the highest possible level of health and safety for aviation squadrons improving unit operational performance and readiness.

(1) FSs and AMSOs shall inform commanding officers on aeromedical factors that may affect operations, readiness, and safety.

(2) FSs shall participate fully in squadron safety functions/boards and human factors boards/councils.

(3) FSs, via aircrew surveillance, shall spend at least 50 percent of their regular duty time directly engaged in aeromedical activities in the squadron spaces.

(4) FSs and AMSOs shall investigate environmental hazards associated with the flight environment and/or aircraft maintenance and assist the ASO in physiologic hazard reporting.

(5) FSs and AMSOs shall assist in the investigation of aircraft mishaps as either full or adjunct members of aircraft mishap boards. Their expertise in aeromedical and physiologic aspects of the flight environment, human factors and aviation life support systems can be a valuable resource to assist the board.

g. Senior Member, Aircraft Mishap Board (AMB)

(1) Senior Member AMB duties are delineated in reference (g).

(2) In the case of Safety Investigation Report (SIR) extensions obtained to await the release of an Engineering Investigation (EI) report, the AMB Senior Member shall not delay the release of the SIR for more than 60 days. Regardless of an outstanding status of an EI, the AMB Senior Member shall release the SIR no later than 90 days from the date of the mishap.

(3) If a SIR is released while an EI is still pending, the AMB Senior Member shall review the EI once published. If the EI report impacts the findings and recommendations of the published SIR, the AMB Senior Member shall notify the current endorser, and release a modified SIR in accordance with reference (g).

4. Mishap Reporting

a. Reporting of defined naval aviation mishaps shall be in accordance with reference (g) except as made more restrictive by this Order.

b. Marine Corps units that use the "TBA, TBD, or UNK" terms specifically authorized by chapter 5 of reference (g) in the mishap classification section of an initial Mishap Data Report (MDR) shall produce an amended MDR providing an estimated damage total and mishap classification within 48 hours of the release of the initial MDR.

c. Squadrons and units experiencing a mishap will apply appropriate cost procedures to obtain an accurate data classification estimate. It is understood that damage classification may not be finalized within the 48 hours allowed. The requirement to later modify an initial mishap classification will not be viewed adversely once due diligence has been applied to the initial estimates.

d. Squadrons and units should not hesitate to request investigation assistance from COMNAVSAFECEN even when using the TBD caveat if, in the judgment of the commander, their investigative assistance is required.

e. All safety message traffic shall include CMC (SD) as an information recipient.

f. Squadrons should not hesitate to contact CMC (SD) with questions or the need for any clarification on the above.

5. Recurring Requirements

    a. ORM Status Report

        (1) The ORM Status Report provides commanders and higher headquarters a visual tool to track the satisfaction of specific aviation related requirements. These requirements represent the minimum acceptable standards for flying squadrons, VMU squadrons, MALS and MAGs. Although it is normally a function of the DOSS to compile and submit the ORM Status Report, satisfaction of all minimum requirements demands close coordination across all departments within the squadrons, groups, wings and MARFORs. Conscious deviations from these requirements must withstand the toughest scrutiny and only be tolerated when these heavily weighted risk decisions are made at the appropriate level.

        (2) To ensure compliance with applicable aviation policies, directives, orders and instructions, all flying commands, detachments and aviation logistics units shall submit this monthly status report to their controlling custodian safety office via the chain of command. Table 3-1 of this Order lists these requirements. To allow adaptation, flexibility and currency of the business rules, CMC (SD) may promulgate exemptions for selected commands and business, as needed.

        (3) Additional requirements which are considered to be minimum acceptable requirements and reported on the ORM Status Report but that are not addressed in this Order are the requirements of the Aviation Commander's Preparation Program as detailed in MARADMIN 270/05, request for NAVSAFECEN survey, Aircraft Maintenance Officer school training and Weapons and Tactics Officer training.

        (4) Report Control Symbol MC-5100-08 is assigned to this reporting requirement.

    b. Safety Climate Surveys. Unit commanders shall ensure the health of the command safety program and the command climate. Safety climate surveys are a valuable tool for assessing each. Satisfaction of this requirement is considered a minimum acceptable requirement and is reported on the ORM Status Report. Report Control Symbol MC-5100-07 is assigned to this reporting requirement.

        (1) All aviation group headquarters (i.e. MAG, Marine Wing Support Group (MWSG), Marine Air Control Group (MACG) and their Personnel Support Detachments) shall conduct the Higher Headquarters (HHQ) survey within 90 days of change of command and annually thereafter. HHQ surveys can be accessed through the "Higher HQ" icon on the GCASS website. The CMC (SD) website contains a button that the user may use to access the GCASS website.

        (2) All flying, Unmanned Aerial System (UAS), MALS and aviation detachments shall conduct a survey to assess the command climate within 30 days of change of command in order to establish a 30-day baseline for the new commander. This survey shall include the below components as applicable to the command:

            (a) The Command Safety Assessment (CSA) addresses squadron safety from the aircrew vantage point – those individuals who operate aircraft. CSA surveys can be accessed through the blue "Aviation Commands Only" icon on the GCASS website. The CMC SD website contains an icon to access the GCASS website.

(b) The Maintenance Climate Assessment Survey (MCAS) obtains feedback on safety climate perceptions from aircraft maintainers. MCAS surveys can be accessed through the blue "Aviation Commands Only" icon on the GCASS website. The CMC SD website contains an icon to access the GCASS website.

(c) The Administrative Support Personnel Assessment (ASPA) survey is available for non-aircrew and non-maintainer personnel within these aviation units and organizational level maintenance units (S-shop personnel who do not fly or perform maintenance). ASPA surveys can be accessed through the "support personnel" icon on the GCASS website. The CMC SD website contains an icon to access the GCASS website.

(3) Commands shall conduct one of the following annually from the date of the last survey, to include the 30-day baseline survey.

(a) Appropriate CSA/MCAS/ASPA surveys (ensure the proper survey is assigned to each division within the squadron).

(b) Culture Workshop.

(c) An informal safety site survey conducted by squadron personnel or by a sister squadron.

(d) A formal NAVSAFECEN Safety Site Survey. If the opportunity presents itself, and the command desires, the command may use a formal NAVSAFECEN survey as a post-change of command baseline survey as long as the 30-day requirement is satisfied.

(4) Any of the above listed surveys shall also be conducted following a change of aircraft model, permanent change of operating base, or a change of significant number of personnel in key billets.

(5) All aviation support squadrons (MWSG squadrons, MACG squadrons, and Marine Wing Headquarters squadrons) shall adhere to the Marine Corps GCASS requirements detailed in chapter 2 of this enclosure.

(6) Aviation commanding officers have the discretion and are encouraged to access, via the GCASS website, a set of ground safety climate surveys to assess the posture of a commander's ground safety programs. Marine squadrons shall access all ground safety climate surveys specifically on the GCASS website. Do not access ground safety climate surveys via the "Aviation Commands Only" icon.

(7) Completion of safety climate surveys are considered a minimum acceptable requirement and are reported on the ORM Status Report.

c. ORM Review Boards

(1) Marine Corps NATOPS Model Managers (MM) shall conduct ORM Review Boards in conjunction with the annual NATOPS conference. A stand alone Marine Corps board will be used for communities with unique missions or Type/Model/Series (T/M/S) aircraft which the Navy does not operate. For

those circumstances in which MM duties and responsibilities reside with a Navy command, a like-T/M/S platform command in the Marine Corps shall act as the Marine Corps MM liaison e.g., VMFAT-101 for F/A-18 A/C/D, MAG-14 for EA-6B, VMR-1 for UC-12/UC-20/UC-35 and collect, correlate, and combine inputs for those platforms and ensure the annual T/M/S NATOPS conference agenda addresses ORM.

(2) The MAW shall ensure squadrons actively participate in the respective T/M/S ORM review boards and leverage Marine Aviation Training System Site (MATSS) as an integral resource to these boards.

(3) The boards will identify improvements outside the squadrons' areas of influence through the review of existing training procedures, T/M/S SOP, Maneuver Description Guides (MDG), and flight briefing guides. To augment existing risk management requirements at these conferences, the NATOPS MM shall:

(a) Determine scope and duration of the board.

(b) Publish via naval message a top ten list of high/blue threat activities within their communities and brief applicable items at their T/M/S Operational Advisory Group (OAG).

d. ORM Safetygrams

(1) Safetygrams are published to identify and address hazards and risk mitigation techniques identified by the fleet for the purpose of awareness and sharing best practices.

(2) Aircraft MMs shall coordinate with their respective squadrons and provide monthly updates in naval message format titled, "ORM SAFETYGRAM", to share community information. These Safetygrams shall include a summary list of mishaps, SIRs, and hazard reports published the previous month from within the community. MMs will forward the Safetygrams to CMC (SD), DC AVN (APP)/(ASM) and COMNAVSAFECEN in addition to other addressees.

(3) Completion of the ORM Safetygram is considered a minimum acceptable requirement for required squadrons and is reported on the ORM Status Report.

e. 14-Day Back Brief

(1) Within 14 days of respective CG MAW SIR endorsement of any Class A or B Flight Mishap, Flight Related Mishap or Aviation Ground Mishap, the MAW CG shall brief the DC AVN on mishap causal factors and corrective action. In the case of a mishap SIR endorsed by multiple MAWs, the MAW CG to which the mishap unit was operationally attached at the time of the mishap will provide the 14-Day Back Brief.

(2) The goal of this brief is to obtain clarity on safety recommendations and corrective actions to share across Marine Aviation. This report does not replace the requirement to submit an 8-day Report to ACMC and DC AVN per this Order.

(3) Coordinate briefs with the DC AVN Executive Assistant (EA). The brief is face-to-face or video teleconference with an accompanying information paper or slide presentation. When deemed appropriate, such as

cases where causal factors are purely material or beyond the influence of any Marine Corps activity, the Wing CG delivering the brief may request an alternate delivery method when coordinating for the delivery of the brief.

   f. Aviation Safety Council

       (1) Squadrons, air stations and other large aviation commands shall form an Aviation Safety Council (ASC) per reference (g). The council will set goals, manage assets, review safety-related recommendations, and keep records of their meetings.

       (2) ASCs are required to meet quarterly.

       (3) The council, with the ASO, GSO and the unit FS or AMSO as permanent members, should review command plans, policies, procedures, conditions, and instructions to ensure currency, correctness, and responsiveness to safety recommendations. Membership may also include the XO, the Quality Assurance Officer, the Aviation Ordnance Officer and the Flight Line Officer. Composite squadrons shall also include the detachment officer-in-charge (OIC) or other representative from each detachment.

       (4) Minutes from the meeting shall be routed for endorsement, comment, and action to all levels of the command including the CO. The ASO shall ensure the minutes are published and disseminated to all aircrew.

       (5) The CO shall ensure aviation detachments not co-located with the squadron are included in the squadron's ASC or may elect to delegate these duties to the detachment commander.

       (6) The ASC is considered a minimum acceptable requirement and is reported on the ORM Status Report.

   g. Enlisted Aviation Safety Committee (EASC)

       (1) Flying squadrons and MALS shall form an EASC. The EASC shall identify and review safety deficiencies and make recommendations for improving safety practices and awareness. Membership shall include, but is not limited to, enlisted representatives from every work center in the command.

       (2) EASCs are required to meet monthly.

       (3) Minutes from the meeting shall be routed for endorsement, comment, and action to all levels of the command including the CO. The Enlisted NATOPS NCO or Aviation Safety Specialist shall ensure the minutes are published and disseminated to all aircrew and maintenance personnel.

       (4) The CO shall ensure aviation detachments not co-located with the squadron are included in the squadron's EASC or may elect to delegate the EASC duties to the detachment commander.

       (5) The EASC is considered a minimum acceptable requirement and is reported on the ORM Status Report.

h. Standardization Board

(1) Shall review flight maneuver execution within the squadron/unit to ensure standardization and that flight operations are in accordance with the appropriate Maneuver Description Guides (MDG), NATOPS, and squadron SOP. The Standardization Board shall ensure all personnel with instructor designations are held to the most rigorous performance and conduct standards. When such an individual or crew is not in compliance with standards, the board will recommend corrective actions to the CO.

(2) Shall recommend approval of new flight designations to the CO, review previous designations of all members of the command, and review current selection and designation requirements.

(3) Membership, at a minimum, will consist of the XO, DOSS, Operations Officer, ASO, NATOPS Officer, Weapons and Tactics Instructor (WTI), unit Flight Leadership Standardization Evaluator (FLSE), and Weapons and Tactics Crew Chief Instructor, where applicable, and FS. Composite squadrons shall include the detachment OIC or other representative from each detachment.

(4) Contract Instructors (CI) shall be Standardization Board members at Fleet Replacement Squadrons (FRS) and should be included as squadron standardization board members for non-FRS squadrons. Marine Aviation Training System Site (MATSS) officers-in-charge at each Marine Corps Air Station shall ensure standardization of CI per Training and Readiness Programs of Instruction (POI), T/M/S and other Marine Corps directives.

(5) The CO shall make comments on published minutes ensuring a formalized feedback loop (e.g., read and initial board) is used and all aircrew have read the final Standardization Board results.

(6) Active duty squadron Standardization Boards are required to meet monthly; reserve squadrons are required to meet quarterly.

(7) The CO shall ensure aviation detachments not co-located with the squadron are included in the squadron's Standardization Board or may elect to delegate the Standardization Board duties to the detachment commander.

(8) The Standardization Board is considered a minimum acceptable requirement and is reported on the ORM Status Report.

i. Human Factors Council (HFC)

(1) The HFC shall be a non-punitive forum used to evaluate an individual's current level of training, qualification progress, flight discipline, and job performance. The HFC shall review the personal and professional characteristics of all aircrew that fly regularly in squadron aircraft. The HFC shall include, at a minimum, the CO or XO, ASO, Operations Officer, Training Officer, NATOPS Officer and the FS. Composite squadrons shall include the detachment officer-in-charge or other representative from each detachment.

(2) Active duty squadron HFCs are required to meet monthly; reserve squadron HFCs are required to meet quarterly.

(3) HFC reports, notes, materials or other work product shall only be available to and retain by the CO or Human Factors Board and shall be treated as For Official Use Only (FOUO). Carefully protect this information against inappropriate disclosure and retained until the subject aircrew or the CO transfers, or they are deemed no longer relevant. This information is only for the CO's use and enhancement of safety; it shall be kept in confidence, and not be used for disciplinary or administrative action.

(4) The CO shall ensure aviation detachments not co-located with the squadron are included in the squadron's HFC or he may elect to delegate the HFC to the detachment commander.

(5) The HFC is considered a minimum acceptable requirement and is reported on the ORM Status Report.

j. Human Factors Board (HFB)

(1) HFBs are an administrative, formal review of all known factors potentially affecting the ability of an individual to perform aircrew responsibilities in a safe and efficient manner. The HFB shall identify specific problem(s) and provide a course of action for resolution. A formal report with conclusions and recommendations should be produced and forwarded to the CO for determination of final action. HFBs are non-punitive and results shall not be used for disciplinary action.

(2) COs shall convene an HFB whenever the ability of an aircrew to safely perform flight duties is in question. Normal board composition includes the XO (chairman), an ASO School graduate, FS and another experienced officer. In the event an enlisted crew member is the subject of the HFB, a senior enlisted crew member shall be included.

k. Instrument Flight Board. Squadrons may be required to maintain an Instrument Flight Board. The members of this board are charged with conducting instrument evaluations. Instrument flight procedures or standardization issues or concerns not adjudicated by the Standardization Board shall be forwarded for resolution to the Instrument Flight Board.

Operational Risk Management Status Report

Status Elements	Requirement	Reference	Background	Notes
Change of Command	Directed	N/A	N/A	N/A
30 Day Command Survey Baseline	Within 30 days of Change of Command	MCO 5100.29B	Determine baseline command climate.	N/A
Annual Command Survey	12 months of baseline survey	MCO 5100.29B OPNAVINST 3750.6R	Determine command climate.	N/A
Human Factors Council	Monthly for active component / Quarterly for reserve component	MCO 5100.29B OPNAVINST 3750.6R	Review of the physical condition, psychological well-being, attitude and motivation of aircrew and squadron personnel.	N/A
Standardization Board	Monthly for active component / Quarterly for reserve component	MCO 5100.29B	Discuss standardization within the squadron and maintain selection and qualification process of aircrew.	N/A
Enlisted Aviation Safety Committee	Monthly	OPNAVINST 3750.6R MCO 5100.29B	Discuss safety deficiencies and provide recommendations for improving safety practices and awareness.	N/A
Aviation Safety Council	Quarterly	MCO 5100.29B	Review command plans, policies, procedures, conditions and instructions to ensure their currency, correctness and responsiveness to safety recommendations.	N/A
Maintenance Inspection	Annual for FRS / 24-30 months for deploying units	OPNAVINST 4790.2H	Ensure maintenance is being conducted as per instruction.	N/A
NATOPS Inspection	18 months	OPNAVINST 3710.7U	Ensure squadron and aircrews are adhering to NATOPS procedures and requirements.	N/A
Naval Safety Center Survey	Biennial	OPNAVINST 3750.6R MCO 5100.29B	Identify organizational strengths and potential hazards, which are often the results of a unit's culture.	N/A

Figure 3-1.--Operational Risk Management Status Report

CO Execute Orders	6 months prior to Change of Command	MARADMIN 270-05	Ensure officers slated for command complete appropriate aviation and aviation command related training prior to assuming command.	COs are required to report to gaining Wing or Command 6 months prior to assuming command.
CO's Flight Training	Prior to Change of Command	MARADMIN 270-05	Ensure officers slated for command complete appropriate aviation flight training prior to assuming command.	CO must complete prerequisite flight training, refresher, conversion training for aircraft to be flown during command.
CMC Commanders Course	Prior to Change of Command	MARADMIN 270-05	Ensure officers slated for command complete appropriate aviation command related training prior to assuming command.	Complete prior to CO assuming command.
CO Aviation Safety Commanders Course	Prior to Change of Command	OPNAVINST 3750.6R	Ensure officers slated for command complete appropriate aviation command related training prior to assuming command.	Complete prior to CO assuming command.
Aviation Maintenance Officers Course	As per OPNAVINST	OPNAVINST 4790.2H Vol. 1	Ensure officers assigned complete appropriate training prior to assuming billet.	Complete within 60 days of assuming the billet.
Aviation Safety Officers Course	As per OPNAVINST	OPNAVINST 3750.6R MCO 5100.29B	Ensure officers assigned complete appropriate training prior to assuming billet.	Complete prior to assuming the billet.
Weapons and Tactics Instructor Course	As per MCO	MCO 3500.109	Ensure continuity of WTI training with in the squadron.	N/A
Monthly Safety Gram Message	Monthly	MCO 5100.29B	Pass best safety practices to fleet squadrons and a recap of HAZREPS and SIRs.	Submitted to FRS by fleet squadrons.

Figure 3-1.--Operational Risk Management Status Report--Continued

Chapter 4

Warrior Preservation Status Report (WPSR) Instructions

1. WPSR Purpose. The WPSR is a measurement tool to assist the commander monitor the strength of the chain of command's safety program and the safety status at a glance. The WPSR provides commanders and higher headquarters a visual tool to track the satisfaction of specific ground safety requirements. This chapter lists the reporting elements and specifies the business rules associated with each one. These elements reflect minimum acceptable standards for a command to operate safely and effectively. As such, it is expected that each command will take the necessary actions to bring each element into the green and maintain it there.

2. Reporting Requirements. Each MARFOR, LOGCOM, MCRC and MCCDC shall collect reports from subordinate commands, brief their appropriate commander, and send a consolidated report to CMC SD no later than 15 January, 15 April, 15 July, and 15 October each year.

3. WPSR Template Location. The WPSR template is published on CMC SD web site. Report Control Symbol is MC-5100-05.

4. WPSR Business Rules

    a. Table 1 provides criteria and instructions to complete the quarterly WPSR. Do not edit, add, modify formats, change or delete cells, columns or rows of the WPSR. Do not over-write or modify any formulas in the WPSR. Formats are locked and will not accept entries that are not in the correct format. Enter dates (MM/DD/YYYY), numbers or percentages as requested. Do not make text entries except to answer deployed question on the spreadsheet. Certain cells are conditionally formatted and will change background color based on entered data. Generally, the color formatting conditions are unique to each reporting element.

        Green meets minimum prescribed criteria

        Yellow marginal compliance or requires attention

        Red fails to meet criteria

        Black not applicable

    b. The following terms are defined as:

        (1) Annual = 365 days

        (2) Semi-annual = 180 days

        (3) Quarterly = 3 calendar months

        (4) Monthly = 30 days

5. <u>Scoring</u>. Scoring is based on the degree to which the unit meets criteria for reported elements. Scores are aggregated to higher level commands. The number of mishaps and open hazards assigned Risk Assessment Codes of 1, 2 or 3 are not scored. A deployed unit's data is not scored or aggregated by higher commands.

Warrior Preservation Status Report

Status Elements	Data	Requirement	Reference	Background	Notes
Change of Command	Date	Directed	N/A	N/A	Enter date in which the current Commanding Officer assumed command.
Deployed	Yes/No	N/A	N/A	Used to determine non-applicability of certain requirements	Select Y or N from the drop down list. Deployed units are encouraged to maintain safety programs and enter data while deployed, but the data will not be scored by the higher commands while the unit is in a deployed status.
Unit Strength	Number Military & Civilian	N/A	N/A	Used to determine non-applicability of certain requirements	Enter the number of Military and Civilians assigned to the Unit.
Command Climate Survey	Date	Initial/Annual	MCO 5100.29B, 4.b.(13)(c)	Commanders will complete Command Climate Survey upon assumption of Command and annually thereafter.	Higher headquarters survey required within 90 days of assumption of command; 05 and 06 commanders complete CCS within 90 days of assumption of command. Once an annual survey is conducted, the annual status over-rides the 90 day requirement. Available on CMC SD web site. GREEN = CCS within 30 days of COC within 1 year of last survey YELLOW = CCS within 60 days of COC or less than 1 quarter overdue RED = No CCS within 90 days of COC or more than 2 quarters overdue
Command Safety Council	Date	Quarterly	NAVMC Dir 5100.8, 4001	Council shall meet on a regular basis, at least quarterly or more frequently as directed by the chairperson.	Commands <500 personnel shall participate in the host installation safety council. GREEN = Held within Quarter YELLOW = Held within Quarter plus 1 Month RED = Not Held within Quarter plus 1 Month If your unit participated in the local installation/base/station host commands safety council, enter that date.

Figure 4-1.--WPSR criteria and instructions

Safe Driving Council	Date	Quarterly	MCO 5100.19E, Para. 1. a.6, Encl (1)	Safe Driving Council shall meet quarterly or more frequently if circumstances warrant.	Commands <500 personnel shall participate in the host installation safe driving council. GREEN = Held within Quarter YELLOW = Held within Quarter plus 1 Month RED = Not Held within Quarter plus 1 Month If your unit participated in the local installation/base/station host command safe driving council, enter that date.
Workplace Safety Inspection	Date Complete	Annual	NAVMC Dir 5100.8, 7003	All workplaces on the installation including tenant commands shall be inspected at least annually by installation SOH personnel.	While this is a core safety service provided by bases and installations, all commanders shall track completion inspections at their location. Color coding is based on the date facilities were last inspected. GREEN = inspected within the last year. YELLOW = inspected within the last year plus 1 month. RED = not inspected within the last year plus 1 month.
ORM Training	% Complete Overall	Initial/Annual	MCO 3500.27B, Para. 5 (a) and (c)	(a): Provide initial and annual refresher training on the process of ORM to all unit personnel. (c:) Document ORM training in member's training record.	Enter % complete. Enter % of unit's on-hand strength that have completed the training as of the end of Quarter (WPSR Reporting) date. GREEN = 95% or better trained YELLOW = 75% or better trained (1 quarter behind) RED = less than 75% trained
Supervisor Safety Training	% Complete Overall	Initial/Annual	NAVMC Dir 5100.8, Para. 5001 (5) and (6)	(5): ISMs and safety officers shall ensure SOH training is provided to all supervisory personnel. New supervisors shall be provided the training within 90 days of appointment. (6): ISMs and safety officers shall ensure supervisors receive annual training that is a refresher and update to their initial supervisors' safety training.	Enter % complete. Enter % of unit's on-hand strength that have completed the training as of the end of Quarter (WPSR Reporting) date. GREEN = 95% or better trained YELLOW = 75% or better trained (1 quarter behind) RED = less than 75% trained

Figure 4-1.--WPSR criteria and instructions--continued

Ground Safety for Marines Trained	Date	Appoint in writing	MCO 5100.29B, Encl (1), Chap 2, para 2 d (1)	Appoint, in writing, a unit safety officer as a special staff officer with direct access to the commander and executive officer for safety matters.	Enter date the Ground Safety Officer/Manager was appointed and the date of Ground Safety for Marines (GSM) completion. GREEN = GSO Trained within 90 days of appointment YELLOW = GSO Trained within 90 days of appointment plus 1 month RED = GSO not trained within 90 days of appointment plus 1 month ** DO NOT ENTER A "TRAINED" DATE WITHOUT AN APPOINTMENT DATE **

Operational Pauses	Date	Semiannual	MCO 5100.29B, 4.b.(13)(e) and Encl (1), Chap 2, para 2 f	Ensure operational pauses are held at least semiannually.	Operational Pauses are held semi-annually Back-in-the-saddle (BITS) follow extended winter holidays or post-deployment. BITS may serve as one of the semi-annual Op Pauses. Complete once, every 6 months. Enter date of most recent training.
					GREEN = Within 6 months of COC #OR# Within 6 months of end of quarter
					YELLOW = Within 7 months of COC #OR# not more than 1 Month overdue
					RED = Not within 7 Months of COC #OR# More than 1 month overdue

Mishaps Class A	Number	A running total	MCO P5102.1B, 2002 (1)	The resulting total cost of damages to DoD or non-DoD property in an amount of $2 million or more; a DoD aircraft is destroyed; or an injury and/or occupational illness result in a fatality or permanent total disability.	Insert the Number of Class A Mishaps this Quarter and running total for calendar year, i.e., 0 / 2. This item is color coded but is not scored.
Mishaps Class B	Number	A running total	MCO P5102.1B, 2002 (2)	The resulting total cost of damages to DoD or non-DoD property is $500,000 or more, but less than $2 million. An injury and/or occupational illness result in permanent partial disability or when three or more personnel are hospitalized for inpatient care (beyond observation) as a result of a single mishap.	Insert the Number of Class B Mishaps this quarter and running total for calendar year, i.e., 0 / 2. This item is color coded but is not scored.

Figure 4-1.--WPSR criteria and instructions--continued

Mishaps Class C	Number	A running total	MCO P5102.1B, 2002 (3)	The resulting total cost of damages to DoD or non-DoD property is $50,000 or more, but less than $500,000; a non-fatal injury that causes any loss of time from work beyond the day or shift on which it occurred; or a nonfatal occupational illness that causes loss of time from work or disability at any time.	Insert the Number of Class C Mishaps this quarter and running total for calendar year, i.e., 0 / 2. This item is not color coded or scored.
Number Motorcycle Riders (Sportbike and Other)	Number	Capture unit riding population.	MCO 5100.19E	Commands will maintain a running survey of motorcycle riders.	Enter the number of Marines identified as Sport Bike Riders by Unit Diary Entry Code A5, or as other motorcycle riders by Unit Diary Entry Code A6. A Rider is a person who owns or regularly rides a motorcycle. Marines who own but do not maintain a motorcycle at their duty station are considered "riders." Marines who have indicated an intention to purchase a motorcycle are not considered "riders."

Figure 4-1.--WPSR criteria and instructions--continued

Required Motorcycle Training Completed	Number	Percentage (# trained/total riders per class of motorcycle)X 100	MCO 5100.19E, Encl. (2) Para. (2) b	Operators of government or privately owned motorcycles, mopeds, motor scooters, or ATVs must successfully complete a rider or operator course prior to operation on any DoD installation.	All Riders, plus Marines indicating an intention to obtain a motorcycle are required to take the MSF Basic Riders Course (BRC). Upon completion record Unit Diary Entry Code M1. Sport Bike riders must attend the MSF Military Sport Bike Rider Course (MSRC) and other riders must attend the Experience Rider Course (ERC) within 120 days of BRC and every three years thereafter. Upon completion, record Unit Diary Entry Code M2 for MSRC and M3 for ERC. Every three years, all motorcycle riders must attend refresher training. Enter the number of riders reflecting Unit Diary Codes showing they completed BRC, MSRC, or ERC. Color coding for the BRC, MSRC, and ERC columns is based on the percentage of riders that have met the respective requirements. BRC ; MSRC; ERC ; Recurring - MSRC or ERC; GREEN Number Trained >= 95% of Total Riders 95% of Sport Bike Riders 95% of Other Riders 95% Within 3 Years YELLOW Number Trained >= 80% of Total Riders 80% of Sport Bike Riders 80% of Other Riders 80% Within 3 Years RED Number Trained < 80% of Total Riders 80% of Sport Bike Riders 80% of Other Riders 80% Within 3 Years Alternative Refresher Training may be submitted to CMC SD for consideration.
Motorcycle Advanced Training for Mentors	Number	Percentage (# trained/total riders per class of motorcycle)X 100	MCO 5100.19E	Each Battalion/Squadron level command shall establish a Motorcycle Club and have two riders complete advanced training for the purpose of mentoring less experienced riders.	Only applicable to BN/SN level units with motorcycle club. Acceptable Advanced Courses include the Keith Code "AMOS" or Lee Parks Total Control. Other curricula may be submitted to CMC SD for consideration. Number of Marines with UD Code M4 GREEN = Number Trained >= 2 YELLOW = Number Trained >= 1 RED = Number Trained = 0
Driver Awareness Training (DAT)	Number	Percentage (# trained/total requiring DAT)X 100	MCO 5100.19E Encl (2) 3. b. (chg. 3)	Required for all Marines 26 Years and younger.	Obtain # Marines untrained frm Admin/Training (S3) GREEN = Number Trained >= 95% of Marines 26 & Under YELLOW = Number Trained >=80% of Marines 26 & Under RED = Number Trained <80% of Marines 26 & Under For Calculation Purposes, Number of Marines 26 & under is assumed at 75% of Military population.

Figure 4-1.--WPSR criteria and instructions--continued

Seatbelt Usage Report	% Usage	Annual	MCO 5100.19E, Encl 2 Para.14 (m)	Installation commanders shall submit an Annual Safety Belt Usage Report no later than 15 February of each year to CMC SD.	Enter % of personnel who are using their seatbelts while on base during the quarter.
Industrial Hygiene Survey	Date	Frequency Varies with intensity of industrial activity	NAVMC DIR 5100.8, chap 11,	Industrial hygiene professionals determine frequency of survey from risk assessments per NMCPHC Technical Manual 6990-91_2, Rev B, Industrial Hygiene Field Operations Manual.	Enter most recent date.
Risk Assessment Code (RAC) - 1	Number	Percentage (# RAC 1 outstanding/ total RAC 1s)X100	NAVMC 5100.8CH 77006, 7007 and 7008	Number of RAC-1 are tracked by Installation Safety Office and should be cleared within 30 days.	Applies only to installations providing core safety services. Insert the Number of RAC-1 Findings over 30 days old as of End of Quarter (WPSR Reporting) date. This item is not color-coded or scored.
Risk Assessment Code (RAC) - 2	Number	Percentage (# RAC 2 outstanding/ total RAC 2s)X100	NAVMC 5100.8 CH 7 7006, 7007 and 7008	Number of RAC-2 are tracked by Installation Safety Office and should be cleared within 30 days.	Applies only to installations providing core safety services. Insert the Number of RAC-2 Findings over 30 days old as of End of Quarter (WPSR Reporting) date. This item is not color-coded or scored.
Risk Assessment Code (RAC) - 3	Number	Percentage (# RAC 3 outstanding/ total RAC 3s)X100	NAVMC 5100.8 CH 7 7006, 7007 and 7008	Number of RAC-3 are tracked by Installation Safety Office and should be cleared within 30 days.	Applies only to installations providing core safety services. Insert the Number of RAC-3 Findings over 30 days old as of End of Quarter (WPSR Reporting) date. This item is not color-coded or scored.

Figure 4-1.--WPSR criteria and instructions--continued

Chapter 5

Operational Risk Management (ORM)

1. <u>ORM Process</u>. Risk management is a decision making tool used by personnel at all levels to increase one's awareness of risk by identifying and assessing the potential for loss. Risk management tools are safety tools as well as they are for the ORM process. A sound safety program requires use of both principles and processes of risk management. Risk management enables the user to effectively manage risks and increases the ability to make informed decisions via a systematic process. Ultimately, reducing the potential for loss increases the probability of success as well as safety. Commands shall foster a culture that fully incorporates safety risk management in all on and off duty activities.

2. <u>ORM Principles</u>. ORM incorporates four over-arching principles containing a 5-step process based upon three levels of conditions.

   a. Accept Risk When Benefits Outweigh The Cost. The U.S. Marine Corps tradition is built upon principles of seizing the initiative and taking decisive action. The goal of ORM is not to eliminate risk, but to manage the risk so the mission can be accomplished with the minimum amount of loss.

   b. Accept No Unnecessary Risk. The acceptance of risk does not equate to the imprudent willingness to gamble. Take only risks that are necessary to accomplish the mission.

   c. Anticipate and Manage Risk By Planning. Risk is more easily controlled when identified early in the planning process.

   d. Make Risk Decisions At The Right Level. Risk decisions are made by the leader directly responsible for the operation. Prudence, experience, judgment, intuition, and situational awareness of leaders directly involved in the planning and execution of the mission are the critical elements in making effective risk decisions. When the leaders responsible for executing a mission determine the risk associated with that mission cannot be controlled at the unit level, or goes beyond the commander's stated intent, they shall elevate the decision to their chain of command.

3. <u>5-Step ORM Process</u>. The 5-step ORM process includes:

   a. Identify Hazards (Step 1). Begin with an outline or chart of the major steps in the operation or scenario (operational analysis, aka safety analysis). Next, conduct a preliminary hazard analysis by listing all of the hazards associated with each step in the operational analysis along with possible causes for those hazards.

   b. Assess Hazards (Step 2). For each hazard identified, determine the associated degree of risk in terms of probability and severity. Although not required, the use of a matrix may be helpful in assessing hazards.

   c. Make Risk Decisions (Step 3). First, develop risk control options. Start with the most serious risk and select controls that will reduce the risk to a minimum consistent with mission accomplishment. With selected controls in place, decide if the residual risk is acceptable and the benefit of the operation outweighs the risk. If risk outweighs benefit or if assistance is required to implement controls, communicate with higher authority in the chain of command.

   d. Implement Controls (Step 4). Controls are measures that can be used to eliminate hazards or reduce the degree of risk. These measures include engineering and administrative controls as well as personal protective equipment.

   e. Supervise (Step 5). Conduct follow-up evaluations of the controls to ensure they remain in place and have the desired effect. Additionally, monitor for changes which may require further ORM and take corrective action when necessary.

4. ORM Details. The ORM process exists on three levels. The decision regarding which of the three levels to use is based upon the situation, proficiency level of personnel, and the amount of time and assets available. While it is preferable to perform a deliberate or in-depth ORM process for all evolutions, the time and resources to do so will not always be available. Individuals, whether on- or off-duty, should be able to employ the time-critical process to make sound and timely decisions. The three levels are as follows.

   a. In-depth. The in-depth level is used when time constraints are not a factor to more thoroughly study the hazards and associated risk in a complex operation or system, or one in which the hazards are not well understood.

   b. Deliberate. This level uses primarily experience and brainstorming to identify hazards and develop controls when available time remaining prior to an event or operation is shortening.

   c. Time-Critical. An "on the run" mental or oral review of the situation using either the five-step process without recording the information on paper and is often all that time will allow. Time-critical risk management (TCRM) is employed by personnel to consider risk while making decisions in a time-compressed situation. TCRM is particularly helpful in choosing the appropriate actions when an unplanned event occurs during the execution of a planned operation or during daily routines both on- and off-duty.

List of Other Applicable Safety Program Policies and Resources

1. 29 CFR 1904, "Recording & Reporting Occupational Injuries and Illnesses," August 12, 2010
2. Office Personnel Management Qualification Standards for General Service Series 0018, "Safety and Occupational Health Management"
3. DOD 1400.25-M, "Department of Defense Civilian Personnel Manual (CPM)," 1 Dec 1996
4. DODI 4000.19, "Interservice and Intragovernmental Support," 9 Aug 1995
5. DODD 5000.01, "The Defense Acquisition System,"November 20, 2007
6. DODI 6055.04, "DOD Traffic Safety Program," April 20,2009
7. DODI 6055.05, "Occupational and Environmental Health (OEH)," 11 Nov 2008
8. DOD 6055.05-M, "Occupational Medical Examinations and Surveillance Manual," 2 May 2007
9. DODI 6055.07, "Accident Investigation, Reporting, and Record Keeping," 3 Oct 2000
10. DODI 6055.12, "Department of Defense Hearing Conservation Program (HCP)," 5 Mar 2004
11. Engineering Manual 385-1-1, US Army Corps of Engineers (USACE) "Safety - Safety and Health Requirements," 15 Sept 2008
12. DOD Mil-Std 882D, "Standard Practice for System Safety," 10 Feb 2000
13. MCO 3500.27B, "Operational Risk Management," 5 May 2004
14. MCO 3570.1B, "Range Safety," 19 May 2003
15. MCO 3710.6R, "Marine Corps Aviation Training System (ATS)," 11 Jun 2008
16. MCO 5040.6H, "Marine Corps Readiness Inspections and Assessments," 18 Mar 2007
17. MCO 5100.8, "Marine Corps Occupational Safety and Health Policy Order," 15 May 2006
18. MCO 5100.19E, "Marine Corps Traffic Safety Order," 29 Dec 2000
19. MCO 5100.30B, "Marine Corps Recreation and Off Duty Safety Program," 29 July 2008
20. MCO P5102.1B, "Navy and Marine Corps Mishap and Safety Investigation Reporting and Recordkeeping Manual," 7 Jan 2005
21. MCO 5104.3B, "Marine Corps Radiation Safety Program," 17 Sept 2011
22. MCO 6200.1E, "Marine Corps Heat Injury Prevention Program," 6 June 2002
23. MCO 6260.1E, "Marine Corps Hearing Conseravation Program," 5 Apr 2000
24. MCO P8020.10B, "Marine Corps Ammunition and Explosives Safety Program," 8 Apr 2009
25. MCO 8023.3A, "Qualification and Certification Programs for Class V Munitions and Explosive Devices,"
26. MCO P1710.30E, "Marine Corps Children, Youth, and Teen Programs," 24 Jun 2004
27. OPNAVINST 3710.7U, Naval Air Training and Operating Procedures Standardization (NATOPS) General Flight and Operating Instruction," 1 Mar 2004
28. OPNAVINST 5100.23G, "Navy Safety and Occupational Health Program Manual," 30 Dec 2005
29. OPNAVINST 5450.180D, "Mission and Functions of the Naval Safety Center," 20 May 2005
30. OPNAVINST 5450.215C, "Mission and Functions of the Bureau of Medicine and Surgery (BUMED)," 23 Jan 2006
31. NAVSEA OP-5, "Ammunition and Explosives Ashore Safety Regulations for Handling, Storage, Production, Renovation, & Shipping," 1 Mar 1995
32. NAVSEA S0402-AA-RAD-010, "Radiation Health Protection Manual"
33. NAVMED P-117, revision of July 2007, "Manual of the Medical Department"

HQMC COORDINATION PAGE

COORDINATION PAGE

STAFF AGENCY	NAME	POSITION	DATE
MARFORCOM	Mr. H. T. Parker Deputy Chief of Staff	Concur w/cmts	28 Oct 10
MARFORPAC	Col J.E. Reilly	Concur w/cmts	13 Oct 10
MARFORRES	Col R. A. Johnson	Concur w/cmts	28 Oct 10
DC AVN	LtCol L. E. Villalobos	Concur w/cmts	07 Jun 10
DC I&L	Col T. J. Keating	Concur w/cmts	13 Apr 11
DC M&RA	Mr. R.P. Winkelhausen	Concur w/cmts	10 Jun 10
LOGCOM	Col Benjamin R. Braden	Concur w/o cmts	12 Oct 10
BUMED	CAPT J. Nelson, USN	Concur w/o cmts	17 Jun 10
MCCDC	Col Royal P. Mortenson Included TECOM	Concur w/cmts	19 Oct 10
MCSC	Ms. Sonata Frederickson	Concur w/o cmts	05 May 10
MARSOC	COL P. M. Warker	Concur w/o cmts	27 Oct 10
COMNAVSAFCEN	Mr. A. Lewis	Concur w/o cmts	17 Jun 10
JAG	Col John Ewers	Concur w/o cmts	07 Oct 10
HS	CAPT M. Olesen, USN	Concur w/o cmts	17 Jun 10
DC PR	Ms. J. St.Onge	Concur w/o cmts	4 Apr 11
DC PP&O	Mr. R. Smith	Concur w/o cmts	8 Apr 11
USMC IG	Mr. C. E. Shelton, Jr.	Concur w/comts	4 Apr 11
ARDB	Ms. W. L. Austin	Concur w/o cmts	09 Sep 10
ARDB	Ms. T. Price	Concur w/cmts	09 Sep 10
ARSF	Ms. G. V. Dolan	Concur w/o cmts	19 Aug 10

CLEARANCE OF PROPOSED ISSUANCE

CLASSIFICATION THIS SHEET ONLY:	CLASSIFICATION OF ATTACHED:	ORIGINATING OFFICE:
UNCLASSIFIED	UNCLASSIFIED	SD (SDO)

DATE SUBMITTED:	DATE RECEIVED:	DATE REQUIRED:
2010-08-12	2010-08-12	2010-08-25

	INITIAL	DATE	DIRECTIVE NUMBER AND SUBJECT:
DIRECTIVES	TP	2010-09-09	MCO 5100.29B_2ndVersion - MARINE CORPS SAFETY PROGRAM
SSIC	TP	2010-09-09	COMPLIANCE REVIEW
REPORTS	WA	2010-09-09	
FORMS			SJA CONCURRED WITH COMMENT ON 8/23/2010.
RECORDS MGMT	TP	2010-06-09	
PA/FOIA	GD	2010-08-19	

REFERENCES (a) SECNAV M-5210.2 (b) MCO 5215.1K (c) SECNAVINST 5216.5D (d) NAVMC 5214.2E (e) SECNAV M-5213.1

ITEMS MARKED BELOW INDICATE ERRORS IN THE PROPOSED ADMINISTRATIVE ISSUANCE

☐ 1. Standard Subject Identification Code (SSIC) incorrect or unsuitable. Suggest using *(Ref a)*

☐ 2. Letterhead must be in compliance with references (b) and (c).

☐ 3. Add "FROM" line. Add "TO" line. *(Ref b)*

☐ 4. When referencing DOD issuances, include the Title and date.

☐ 5. Use latest suffix letter when citing instructions. Do not use "series." *(Ref b)*

☐ 6. If reference(s) have not been distributed to all addressees, add the abbrevation "NOTAL" enclosed in parentheses at the end of the reference line. *(Ref c)*

☐ 7. Type subject line in all "CAPITAL" letters.

☒ 8. Title and underline major paragraphs. *(Ref b)*. Paragraph format is incorrect *(Ref b)*.

☒ 9. Remove punctuation after headings when not followed by text.

☐ 10. Type directives identification block data to include originator's office code *(Ref b)*

☐ 11. Allow an extra line below the directives identification to allow for date signed insertion.

☐ 12. Make purpose or situation paragraph a synopsis of the directive's content. *(Ref b)*

☒ 13. Distribution format incorrect/Publications Control Number (PCN) missing *(Ref b)*

☐ 14. Misspellings/typographical errors exist, please proofread.

☐ 15. Route to ARDE to obtain PCN number

☐ 16. Label enclosures. *(Ref b)*

☐ 17. All references and enclosures must be cited in the basic instruction. *(Ref b)*

☐ 18. Use sex-neutral and clear language. *(Refs c)*

☐ 19. Change MCO into the 5 paragraph Order format. *(Ref b)*.

☐ 20. Changes too extensive. Issue a revision.

☐ 21. Pen changes not allowed. Page replacement required for HQMC Directives *(Ref b)*

☐ 22. Bulletins cannot remain in effect for longer than 1 year.

☐ 23. Complete NAVMC 11216/11217 (attached) for each reporting requirement *(Ref d)*

☐ 24. Insufficient time to prepare report.

☐ 25. RCS assigned.

☐ 26. For each report include the report control symbol (report title, location of the report in the directive, and the expiration of the report or the exemption authority.)

☐ 27. For each form include the form number, title, stock number (if applicable) and stocking information. *(Ref e)*

☐ 28. All forms must have a form number. Complete one copy of DD 67(attached) for each form. *(Ref e)*

☐ 29. Filled-in samples of forms must have the word "SAMPLE" overlayed or printed on them. *(Ref e)*

☐ 30. The statement "to be reproduced locally" cannot be used for forms stocked. Contact Marine Corps Form Manager or go to Navy Forms On-line at https://forms.daps.dla.mil for stocking information.

☒ 31. See additional comments attached.

THIS ISSUANCE IS	COMMENTS:
☐ APPROVED	- All acronyms should be in compliance with references (e), (h), and (l) of MCO 5215.1K and spelled out the first time used . Non-compliant acronyms are not recommended.
☒ APPROVED SUBJECT TO MARK-UP / COMMENTS	-- All comments in the compliance review library must be add and/or incorporated into this Order prior to resubmitting for signature.
☐ DISAPPROVED *(When corrections are made, return for approval.)*	- This Order is approved pending the Commandant's Legal (CL's) and comments.
☒ A MARKED UP COPY IS ATTACHED	

SIGNATURE AND TITLE	DATE
PRICE. TONYA.1229538604 — Digitally signed by PRICE.TONYA.1229538604 DN: c=US, o=U.S. Government, ou=DoD, ou=PKI, ou=USMC, cn=PRICE.TONYA.1229538604 Date: 2010.09.09 07:54:46 -04'00'	2010-06-09

Publishing Reminders for HQMC only:
Prior to returning this Order/Directive to HQMC ARDB Directives for publishing do the following:
1. Type date the directive was signed under the directive identification on the upper right on all pages of unclassified directives. Classified and printed directives identification will alternate upper right corner on even pages and upper left corner on odd pages.
2. On classified Orders/Directives type classification at the center top and bottom of each page in the header and footer.

NAVMC HQ 942 (05-07)   [Reset Form]

Adobe Designer 8.0

www.ingramcontent.com/pod-product-compliance
Lightning Source LLC
Chambersburg PA
CBHW080615290526

45790CB00007B/2789